Easy Quilts
from Precut Fabrics

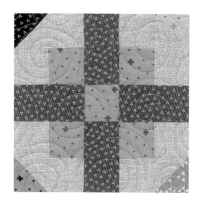

SUE PFAU

of Sweet Jane's Quilting & Design

Martingale®
Create with Confidence

Easy Quilts from Precut Fabrics
© 2018 by Sue Pfau

Martingale®
19021 120th Ave. NE, Ste. 102
Bothell, WA 98011-9511 USA
ShopMartingale.com

Printed in China
22 21 20 19 18   8 7 6 5 4 3 2 1

Library of Congress Cataloging-in-Publication Data is available upon request.

ISBN: 978-1-60468-866-5

MISSION STATEMENT

We empower makers who use fabric and yarn to make life more enjoyable.

CREDITS

PUBLISHER AND CHIEF VISIONARY OFFICER
Jennifer Erbe Keltner

CONTENT DIRECTOR
Karen Costello Soltys

MANAGING EDITOR
Tina Cook

ACQUISITIONS EDITOR
Karen M. Burns

TECHNICAL EDITOR
Ellen Pahl

COPY EDITOR
Melissa Bryan

DESIGN MANAGER
Adrienne Smitke

PRODUCTION MANAGER
Regina Girard

COVER AND INTERIOR DESIGNER
Kathy Kotomaimoce

PHOTOGRAPHER
Brent Kane

ILLUSTRATOR
Sandy Huffaker

Contents

Introduction

My dad always said that a journey of a thousand miles starts with one step. It's a nice phrase to have in the back of your mind, because not every journey or task in life is easy, but you have to start somewhere. If you persevere, you'll reach your destination! When I got the idea to develop a book of patterns for precuts using classic quilt blocks, the task seemed overwhelming. Where do I start? Is it even possible? So I began with one block, and then two, and eventually I had a bunch of different blocks using just my precut squares and strips. Little did I know the possibilities would be endless, and the quilts would be so pretty!

I really like the look of vintage quilts, but I have to say, they usually seem complicated and time consuming—more difficult than I am prepared to tackle. The quilts in this book are simplified versions of vintage-style quilts. By using precuts, I've made fabric selection easier and cutting less time consuming. I developed each pattern with the busy quilter in mind. I tried to design quilts that would go together quickly but still have the more complicated look of the quilts from yesteryear that I admire. I've included a variety of sizes and designs so that you have some easy, quick quilts to choose from. Or if you have more time and want a more complicated quilt (but not too complicated!), there are a few of those as well.

Unintentionally, each of these designs turned out to be a one-block quilt! I guess this appeals to my simple tastes. Making a quilt with the same block has several benefits. You can easily change the size of the quilt by making more or fewer blocks. You can also get in the groove of putting the blocks together without constantly referring to the directions. Piecing doesn't become monotonous, because each block has a different color scheme—it's so fun to select the colors and prints and then watch the block come together!

I love working with precuts. They're economical because you are buying just enough fabric to make your quilt. They come in one neat, prepackaged bundle that you can quickly grab at a quilt shop or purchase on the Internet. They require less pressing and cutting when you are preparing to make your quilt. The patterns in this book use one or two precut bundles, plus some neutral background fabric. Just like my first two books, *Quilts from Sweet Jane* and *One Bundle of Fun* (Martingale, 2013 and 2016, respectively), these pages are full of designs that are easy to start and quick to finish!

~Sue

Using and Choosing Fabrics

Precut bundles are already coordinated, so they always look great together in a quilt. Many quilters have a few packs in their closet, and if you don't, you need to go out and buy a bundle of precut fabrics and see how great they are. But before you get started, there are a few things you should know.

Never prewash precuts! You don't want them to shrink, twist, or fray before you sew with them, as their cut dimensions will no longer be accurate. People who prewash are concerned about colors bleeding, but I've washed many quilts made with unwashed precuts and the colors have never run.

The tips of the pinked edges are considered part of the usable fabric, but always measure to make sure. Each piece in your bundle should be cut the same size, so you need to measure just one to find the size of each square or strip. For example, if your 2½"-wide strip is exactly 2½" wide, including the tips of the pinked edges, use the tips of the pinked edges as the edge of your fabric when you're sewing. If your Layer Cake is 10⅛" × 10⅛", don't cut off a 5" strip and think you have two 5"-wide pieces, because one will be 5⅛" wide.

Moda Precuts

Most of the precuts I used in this book are from Moda fabrics. Their precuts are accurately cut, which eliminates extra cutting or problems with your blocks being the wrong size. Moda's Layer Cake and Jelly Roll bundles contain about 40 pieces of fabric. Moda also offers fat-quarter bundles that contain between 27 and 42 fat quarters, depending on the line of fabric. There's so much fabric in the fat-quarter bundles, you can easily have enough for a bed-sized quilt, which makes for quick fabric selection.

Using Your Stash

If you want to use fabrics from your stash instead of precuts, simply cut fabric to the size of the precuts. Or skip that step completely and cut the number and size of squares and strips as directed in the cutting list. I often cut Jelly Roll strips in half so that they measure approximately 2½" × 21", which makes them interchangeable with strips cut from fat quarters. If cutting from your stash, maintain a variety of colors and prints by using at least 12 different fabrics for smaller quilts and 15 to 20 for larger designs.

Choosing Background Fabric

Low-volume fabrics are prints that read as light or almost solid, even though they are printed with a pattern or design. You can use just one low-volume fabric for the background of your entire quilt, or you can combine many different low-volume fabrics to make a busier, more interesting quilt. I love this look, and it is a very traditional style of quiltmaking. Back in the day, women didn't always have the luxury of access to a light solid or a lot of the same print to use in their quilts.

When I use just one fabric for my background, I find that the easiest way to choose the fabric is by using one already in the line of fabric I'm working with. For the quilts in this book, I used a variety of tactics. For The Ties that Bind on page 37, I bought a fat-quarter bundle that contained a lot of low-volume prints. For The Fourth of July on page 17, I was able to find a Moda Layer Cake that was all low-volume prints. That was the best option, because then I had about 30 different prints in one bundle. I got lucky with those two quilts, but if you can't find a bundle of precoordinated background fabric for your project, your stash is the next best place to start. After you

Precut Varieties

Here is a brief rundown of the precuts used in this book, sorted by
name, size of the precut, and the number of pieces per bundle.

Name	Size	Number of Pieces
Layer Cake	10" × 10" squares	20 to 42 squares per bundle
Jelly Roll	2½" × 42" strips	20 to 40 strips per bundle
Charm squares*	5" × 5" squares	22 to 42 squares per bundle
Fat quarters	18" × 21" rectangles (half of a half yard)	Purchase individually or in bundles of varying quantities
Fat eighths**	9" × 21" rectangles	Purchase individually or in bundles of varying quantities

* There are no projects specifically for charm squares, but they can be used in some Layer Cake or Jelly Roll patterns when the cuts are less than 5" in any direction.

** Fat eighths can be cut into three 2½" × 21" strips and used to make some of the Jelly Roll or fat-quarter patterns in this book.

have sorted through and picked out a few good fabrics, go to your local quilt shop and buy a few more prints to round out the bunch. I typically look for cream fabrics that contain bits of the same colors as my main fabric. Recently I have begun collecting low-volume fabrics to keep ready in my stash, because I love the look so much. Light shades of colors already in your quilt also make great neutral background colors, so don't feel you have to stick with creams and whites.

Low-volume fabrics for backgrounds

Managing Lights and Darks

Precut bundles often contain more dark and medium fabrics than lights. Sometimes you will be forced to incorporate light fabrics into parts of your quilt where you need a medium or dark. Light fabric that has a busy print can read as a darker or contrasting fabric, so you can often include those. You can also add a few fabrics from your stash if you need to, or buy a few coordinating fat quarters from the quilt shop. Don't be afraid to steal some fabric from your binding and backing as well. Before you do this, though, be sure to cut and prepare what you need for the quilt and then see what is left over. I find that bundles of batiks are often entirely made up of darker fabrics, so this is less of an issue if you use batiks.

These medium-lights are busy enough to contrast with a low-volume, light background.

Scattered Flight

FINISHED QUILT: 64½" × 80½"
FINISHED BLOCK: 12" × 12"

The Anvil block is an old design and has many variations. Made with modern fabrics, it looks fresh and lively. I love the simplicity of using just two colors in each block. You can make this quilt with two Layer Cake packages and no additional fabric! I wanted to size it generously enough to use as a coverlet for any of the beds you might have in your home, but if you'd like an even bigger version, make more blocks or add a simple one-color border.

Materials

Yardage is based on 42"-wide fabric.

24 matching pairs of Layer Cake squares, 10" × 10", for block backgrounds*
32 Layer Cake squares for anvils, sashing, and border*
⅔ yard of dark blue print for binding
5½ yards of fabric for backing
73" × 89" piece of batting

You will need a total of two matching Layer Cake bundles (80 squares total).

Sorting the Precuts

After you have sorted the Layer Cake bundles into pairs of matching squares as called for in the materials list, choose the fabrics that will make up each block—one square for the "anvil" and two matching squares for the background. Create 24 sets of squares, one set for each of the 24 blocks.

Cutting

All measurements include ¼" seam allowances.

From *each* of the 24 pairs of squares for the background, cut:
3 squares, 5" × 5" (72 total)
3 squares, 4½" × 4½" (72 total)

From 24 of the squares for the anvil, cut:
3 squares, 5" × 5" (72 total)

From the remaining squares and scraps, cut *a total of:*
104 squares, 4½" × 4½"

From the dark blue print, cut:
8 strips, 2½" × 42"

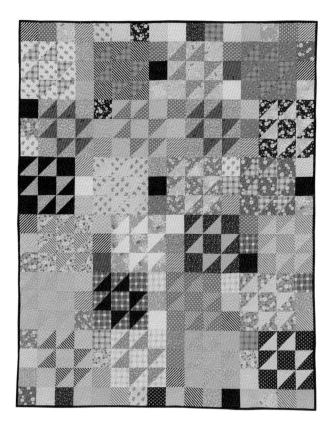

Assembling the Blocks

The instructions are for making one block at a time. Press all seam allowances as shown by the arrows in the illustrations.

1 Draw a diagonal line from corner to corner on the wrong side of the three background 5" squares. Place each marked square right sides together with a contrasting 5" square, aligning the edges. Sew a scant ¼" seam allowance on each side of the marked line on each pair of squares. Cut each pair in half on the drawn line and press. You'll have six identical half-square-triangle units. Trim each unit to measure 4½" square, including seam allowances.

Make 6 units.

Invaluable Half-Square-Triangle Tool

My favorite quilting tool is the Quick Quarter ruler by Quilter's Rule. This tool makes it easy to mark sewing lines when you're making half-square-triangle units from squares. Simply align the center of the ruler with opposite corners on the wrong side of the square and draw a line on each side of the ruler with a pencil. Sew on the marked lines and then cut on the diagonal to make half-square triangles.

2 Arrange the six half-square-triangle units with the three matching 4½" squares as shown. Sew together into rows, and then sew the rows together. The completed block should measure 12½" square, including seam allowances. Make 24 blocks.

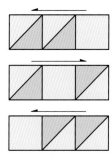 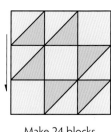

Make 24 blocks,
12½" × 12½".

Assembling the Quilt Top

1 Sew three assorted 4½" squares together to make a sashing unit. Make 24 units that measure 4½" × 12½", including seam allowances.

Make 24 units,
4½" × 12½".

2 Sew four assorted 4½" squares together to make units for the top and bottom border. Make eight border units that measure 4½" × 16½", including seam allowances.

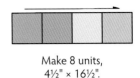

Make 8 units,
4½" × 16½".

3 Arrange the blocks in six rows of four blocks and four sashing units each. In odd-numbered rows, place the blocks so that the seams are all horizontal and facing downward, and place the sashing units so that the seams are all facing upward. In even-numbered rows, place the blocks so that the seams are pressed upward and the sashing seams downward. Sew the blocks into rows, and then join the rows. The quilt center should measure 64½" × 72½", including seam allowances.

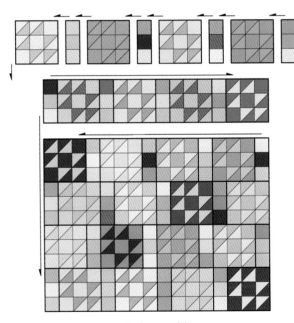

Quilt assembly

4 Sew four border units from step 2 together end to end. Make two border strips.

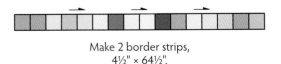

Make 2 border strips,
4½" × 64½".

5 Sew the border strips to the top and bottom of the quilt top. The finished quilt top should measure 64½" × 80½".

Adding borders

Finishing the Quilt

For help with the following steps, go to ShopMartingale.com/HowtoQuilt for free, illustrated instructions.

1 Cut and piece the backing fabric so that it's 4" larger than the quilt top on all four sides.

2 Mark any quilting lines needed, and then layer the backing, batting, and quilt top. Baste the layers together and quilt. The quilt shown was quilted in an overall design of echoing spirals.

3 Trim the batting and backing even with the quilt top.

4 Use the dark blue 2½"-wide strips to make and attach the binding.

Vintage Bear Paw

FINISHED QUILT: 58½" × 72"
FINISHED BLOCK: 6¾" × 6¾"

The Bear Paw block is ubiquitous in vintage quilts and it looks great with any fabric. You can break it up with sashing and cornerstones, set the blocks in many different ways, or use any type of fabric that suits your taste. I love the colorful 1930s prints with just a touch of background fabric thrown in.

Materials

Yardage is based on 42"-wide fabric.

40 Layer Cake squares, 10" × 10", of assorted prints
    for blocks
2½ yards of cream solid for blocks and border
⅝ yard of pink print for binding
4⅛ yards of fabric for backing
67" × 80" piece of batting

Using Light Squares

If some of your Layer Cake squares are light and don't contrast strongly with the background fabric, cut them into 5" squares and use them for the block centers.

Cutting

All measurements include ¼" seam allowances. Choose 20 squares for the block centers and 20 for the half-square triangles and cut as directed.

From *each* of the 20 squares for block centers, cut:
4 squares, 5" × 5" (80 total)

From *each* of the 20 squares for half-square triangles, cut:
8 squares, 3¼" × 3¼" (160 total)

From the cream solid, cut:
14 strips, 3¼" × 42"; crosscut into 160 squares,
    3¼" × 3¼"
6 strips, 2¾" × 42"; crosscut into 80 squares,
    2¾" × 2¾"
7 strips, 2½" × 42"

From the pink print, cut:
7 strips, 2½" × 42"

Resizing the Quilt

I love the size of this quilt, but a smaller version would make a wonderful baby quilt or wall hanging. For a quilt measuring 34¼" × 41", you would need 16 Layer Cake squares and ⅞ yard of background fabric. Cut 8 of the Layer Cake squares into 30 squares, 5" × 5", and cut the other 8 Layer Cake squares into 60 squares, 3¼" × 3¼". This will be enough for 30 blocks, to be arranged in a 5 × 6 block layout. Leave off the 2½" cream border and it will still look great.

Assembling the Blocks

Press all seam allowances as shown by the arrows in the illustrations.

1 Draw a diagonal line from corner to corner on the wrong side of each cream 3¼" square. Place each marked square on a print 3¼" square, right sides together. Sew a scant ¼" seam on each side of the diagonal line. Cut each square in half along the diagonal line and press. Trim each half-square-triangle unit to measure 2¾" square, including seam allowances. Repeat for all 3¼" squares to make a total of 320 units.

Make 320 units.

2 Sort the half-square-triangle units from step 1 into sets of four matching units. Sew them together in sets of two matching units as shown. Make 160 units that measure 2¾" × 5", including seam allowances.

Make 80 of each unit, 2¾" × 5".

3 Arrange two matching units from step 2 with one cream 2¾" square and one contrasting print 5" square as shown. Sew together in rows, and then sew the rows together. The completed block should measure 7¼" square, including seam allowances. Make 80 blocks.

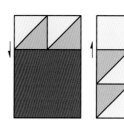 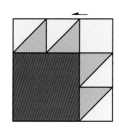

Make 80 blocks, 7¼" × 7¼".

Assembling the Quilt Top

1 Arrange the blocks in 10 rows of eight blocks each, paying close attention to the orientation of the blocks as shown. Make five of row 1 and five of row 2. The same two rows are repeated throughout the quilt.

Audition the Blocks

There are many ways to lay out these blocks, so you may want to experiment with different arrangements before you start sewing things together.

2 Sew the blocks together into rows, and then join the rows. The quilt center should measure 54½" × 68".

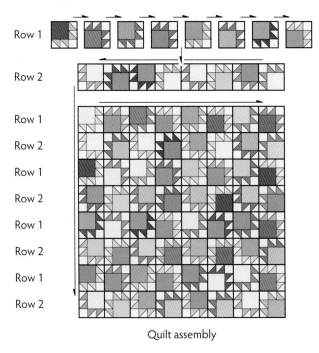

Quilt assembly

3 Join the seven cream 2½" × 42" strips end to end with a diagonal seam to make one long strip. Measure the width of the quilt top through the center and cut two cream strips to this measurement. Sew the strips to the top and bottom of the quilt top. Press the seam allowances toward the center of the quilt.

4 Measure the length of the quilt top through the center and cut two cream strips to that measurement. Sew these strips to the sides of the quilt top. Press the seam allowances toward the center of the quilt. The finished quilt top should measure 58½" × 72".

Finishing the Quilt

For help with the following steps, go to ShopMartingale.com/HowtoQuilt for free, illustrated instructions.

1 Cut and piece the backing fabric so that it's 4" larger than the quilt top on all four sides.

2 Mark any quilting lines needed, and then layer the backing, batting, and quilt top. Baste the layers together and quilt. The quilt shown was quilted in an overall swirl design with flowers stitched randomly throughout.

3 Trim the batting and backing even with the quilt top.

4 Use the pink 2½"-wide strips to make and attach the binding.

The Fourth of July

Layer-Cake Friendly

FINISHED QUILT: 65½" × 81½"
FINISHED BLOCK: 8" × 8"

This quilt goes together surprisingly fast. The King's Crown block appears to be set on point, but it's not! I love how the repetition of one simple block can create secondary designs within a quilt, elevating it to something that appears much more interesting and complex. The simple cream border adds a modern touch and also serves to calm down this busy quilt.

Materials

Yardage is based on 42"-wide fabric.

63 Layer Cake squares, 10" × 10", of red and blue prints for blocks
32 Layer Cake squares of cream prints for blocks*
1¼ yards of cream print for border
⅔ yard of navy print for binding
5½ yards of fabric for backing
74" × 90" piece of batting

*Or substitute 2½ yards of cream print for a less scrappy quilt.

Scrappy Backgrounds Made Easy!

You can find Layer Cakes that are meant to be used exclusively as low-volume background fabrics. They're great because you can get an amazing variety of prints and textures without the investment of collecting many different lengths of yardage. If you can't find a Layer Cake that fits what you need, you can use 2½ yards of one cream background fabric, or pull the equivalent yardage from your stash.

Cutting

All measurements include ¼" seam allowances. Keep like fabrics together as you cut.

From *each* of the 63 red and blue squares, cut:
1 square, 4½" × 4½" (63 total)
4 squares, 2½" × 2½" (63 matching sets, 252 total)
4 rectangles, 2½" × 4½" (63 matching sets, 252 total)

Continued on page 18

Press all seam allowances as shown by the arrows in the illustrations.

1 Draw a diagonal line from corner to corner on the wrong side of the eight cream 2½" squares. Place a marked square on one end of a 2½" × 4½" rectangle, right sides together. Sew on the diagonal line. Trim the seam allowances to ¼" and press.

2 Place a second marked cream 2½" square on the opposite end of the unit made in step 1, right sides together. Make sure the diagonal line is in the correct position. Stitch, trim, and press to complete a flying-geese unit that measures 2½" × 4½", including seam allowances. Make four matching flying-geese units.

Make 4 matching units, 2½" × 4½".

Continued from page 17

From *each* of the 32 cream squares, cut:
16 squares, 2½" × 2½" (512 total; 8 are extra)*

From the cream print, cut:
8 strips, 5" × 42"

From the navy print, cut:
8 strips, 2½" × 42"

If you are using one background fabric, cut 32 strips, 2½" × 42". Crosscut them into a total of 504 squares, 2½" × 2½".

Assembling the Blocks

The instructions are for making one block at a time. For each block you will need:

- A matching set of 1 square, 4½" × 4½" and 4 squares, 2½" × 2½"

- A set of 4 matching rectangles, 2½" × 4½", that contrast or coordinate with the squares

- 8 matching cream squares, 2½" x 2½"

3 Arrange the 4½" square, the four matching 2½" squares, and the flying-geese units in rows as shown. Sew the units into rows; then sew the rows together. The completed block should measure 8½" square, including seam allowances. Make 63 blocks.

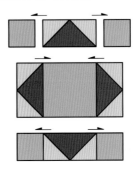 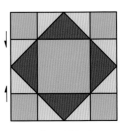

Make 63 blocks, 8½" × 8½".

Assembling the Quilt Top

1 Arrange the blocks in nine rows of seven blocks each. Rotate each block so that the seam allowances go in opposite directions from block to block within each row. Sew the blocks together into rows, and then join the rows.

Quilt assembly

2 Join the cream 5" × 42" strips end to end with a diagonal seam to form one long strip. Measure the length of the quilt top through the center and cut two cream strips to that measurement. Sew the strips to the sides of the quilt top. Press the seam allowances toward the border.

3 Measure the width of the quilt top through the center and cut two cream strips to that measurement. Sew the strips to the top and bottom of the quilt top. Press the seam allowances toward the border. The finished quilt top should measure 65½" × 81½".

Finishing the Quilt

For help with the following steps, go to ShopMartingale.com/HowtoQuilt for free, illustrated instructions.

1 Cut and piece the backing fabric so that it's 4" larger than the quilt top on all four sides.

2 Mark any quilting lines needed, and then layer the backing, batting, and quilt top. Baste the layers together and quilt. The quilt shown was quilted in an overall feather design with swirls.

3 Trim the batting and backing even with the quilt top.

4 Use the navy 2½"-wide strips to make and attach the binding.

Jack's Cross

FINISHED QUILT: 54½" × 54½"
FINISHED BLOCK: 10" × 10"

This quilt, featuring variations of the Crossed Square block, definitely has a more modern feel than some other designs in the book. But with crosses, nine patches, and star points all making an appearance throughout the quilt, it certainly qualifies as traditional! It almost looks like a sampler quilt with two block variations. Different aspects of the blocks become more prominent depending on the color and value placement.

Materials

Yardage is based on 42"-wide fabric.

12 Jelly Roll strips, 2½" × 42", of assorted medium and dark prints for dark blocks
22 Jelly Roll strips of assorted light, medium, and dark prints for block centers and crosses
1⅓ yards of yellow print for light blocks and border
½ yard of navy print for binding
3¾ yards of fabric for backing
61" × 61" piece of batting

Cutting

All measurements include ¼" seam allowances. Keep like fabrics together as you cut.

From *each* of the 12 medium and dark strips for dark blocks (hereafter referred to as darks), cut:
1 strip, 2½" × 10½" (12 total)
4 rectangles, 2½" × 4½" (48 total)

From *each of 13* light, medium, or dark strips for crosses, cut:
8 rectangles, 2½" × 4½" (104 total; 4 are extra)

From *each of 9* light, medium, or dark strips for block centers, cut:
3 strips, 2½" × 10½" (27 total; 2 are extra)
3 squares, 2½" × 2½" (27 total; 2 are extra)

From the leftovers of the medium and dark print strips (hereafter referred to as darks), cut:
72 squares, 2½" × 2½"

From the yellow print, cut:
16 strips, 2½" × 42", crosscut into:
    52 rectangles, 2½" × 4½"
    33 strips, 2½" × 10½"
    4 squares, 2½" × 2½"

From the navy print, cut:
6 strips, 2½" × 42"

Assembling the Blocks

This quilt is made up of 25 blocks: 13 light blocks with yellow frames and 12 dark blocks with dark frames. Set aside 20 of the dark 2½" squares cut from leftovers to use in the border; you'll use the rest in the light blocks, four in each block.

Press all seam allowances as shown by the arrows in the illustrations.

MAKING THE LIGHT BLOCKS

For *each* block framed in yellow, you'll need:

- 1 yellow strip, 2½" × 10½"
- 4 yellow rectangles, 2½" × 4½"
- 1 print strip, 2½" × 10½", and 1 matching print square, 2½" × 2½"
- 4 matching print rectangles, 2½" × 4½"
- 4 dark squares, 2½" × 2½"

1 Sew a yellow 2½" × 10½" strip and a print 2½" × 10½" strip together along the long edges to make a strip set. Crosscut the strip set into four segments, 2½" wide.

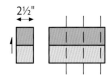

2½"

Make 1 strip set. Cut 4 segments.

2 Sew each segment to a yellow 2½" × 4½" rectangle. Make four units that measure 4½" square, including seam allowances.

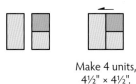

Make 4 units, 4½" × 4½".

3 Arrange the units with the matching print 2½" square and four matching print 2½" × 4½" rectangles as shown. Sew the units into rows, and then sew the rows together. The block should measure 10½" square, including seam allowances.

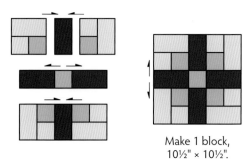

Make 1 block, 10½" × 10½".

Square Up the Block

Before adding the 2½" squares at the corners of the block to make the corner triangles, measure the block and square it up. This makes placing and sewing the 2½" squares onto the finished block much easier!

4 Draw a diagonal line from corner to corner on the wrong side of the four dark 2½" squares. Place a marked square on one corner of the block, right sides together. Sew on the diagonal line. Trim

the seam allowances to ¼" and press. Repeat for each corner. Make 13 light blocks.

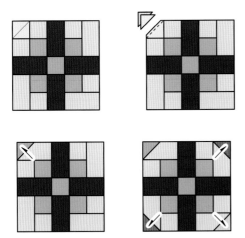

Make 13 blocks.

MAKING THE DARK BLOCKS

For *each* block framed in dark prints, you'll need:

- 1 dark print strip, 2½" × 10½", and 4 matching rectangles, 2½" × 4½"
- 1 print strip, 2½" × 10½", and 1 matching square, 2½" × 2½"
- 4 matching print rectangles, 2½" × 4½"

1 Sew the two print 2½" × 10½" strips together along the long edges to make a strip set. Crosscut the strip set into four segments, 2½" wide.

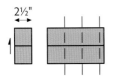

2½"

Make 1 strip set.
Cut 4 segments.

2 Sew each segment to a matching print 2½" × 4½" rectangle. Make four units that measure 4½" square, including seam allowances.

Make 4 units,
4½" × 4½".

3 Arrange the units with the matching print 2½" square and four matching print 2½" × 4½" rectangles as shown. Sew the units into rows, and then sew the rows together. The completed block should measure 10½" square, including seam allowances. Make 12 dark blocks.

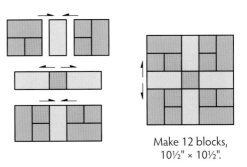

Make 12 blocks,
10½" × 10½".

Assembling the Quilt Top

1 Arrange the blocks in five rows of five blocks each, alternating the light and dark blocks as shown in the assembly diagram. Rotate the blocks as needed so that seams abut. Sew the blocks together into rows and then join the rows.

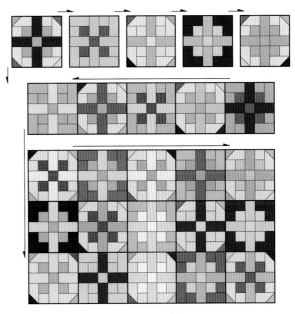

Quilt assembly

2 Draw a diagonal line from corner to corner on the wrong side of the remaining dark 2½" squares. Place a marked square on each end of a yellow 2½" × 10½" strip, right sides together. Sew on the diagonal lines. Trim the seam allowances to ¼" and press. Make eight units that measure 2½" × 10½", including seam allowances.

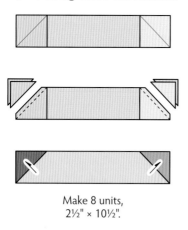

Make 8 units,
2½" × 10½".

3 Place a marked 2½" square on a yellow 2½" square, right sides together. Sew on the diagonal line. Trim the seam allowances to ¼" and press. Make four half-square-triangle units that measure 2½" square, including seam allowances.

Make 4 units,
2½" × 2½".

4 Sew two of the units made in step 2 together with three yellow 2½" × 10½" strips as shown. Make four border strips. Sew a half-square-triangle unit from step 3 to each end of two of the border strips. Do not press the seam allowances yet.

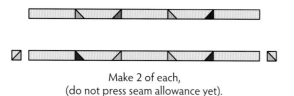

Make 2 of each,
(do not press seam allowance yet).

5 Place the border strips next to the quilt top where they will be added. Press the seam allowances of the border strips in the opposite directions of the seams they will butt up against in the quilt.

6 Sew the top and bottom border strips to the quilt top first, and then add the side border strips. The finished quilt top should measure 54½" square.

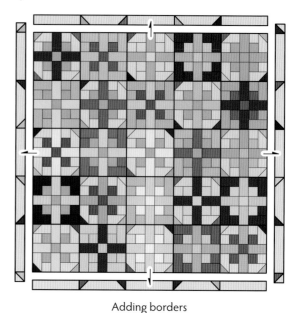

Adding borders

Finishing the Quilt

For help with the following steps, go to ShopMartingale.com/HowtoQuilt for free, illustrated instructions.

1 Cut and piece the backing fabric so that it's 4" larger than the quilt top on all four sides.

2 Mark any quilting lines needed, and then layer the backing, batting, and quilt top. Baste the layers together and quilt. The quilt shown was quilted in an overall spiral design.

3 Trim the batting and backing even with the quilt top.

4 Use the navy 2½"-wide strips to make and attach the binding.

Four Patch Picnic

FINISHED QUILT: 48¼" × 53½"
FINISHED BLOCK: 4" × 4"

Featuring the Four Patch block, this quilt is a good first project for beginners. It's quick, easy, and ideal for smaller Jelly Roll bundles!

Materials

Yardage is based on 42"-wide fabric.

18 Jelly Roll strips, 2½" × 42", of assorted prints for blocks*
1½ yards of cream print for sashing and border
½ yard of lime green solid for binding
3⅛ yards of fabric for backing
55" × 60" piece of batting

After removing selvage ends but before cutting pieces for blocks, measure your strips to make sure you have 41" of usable length. If not, you may need to add strips.

Cutting

All measurements include ¼" seam allowances.

From *each* of the 18 assorted print strips, cut:
4 strips, 2½" × 10¼" (72 total)

From the cream print, cut:
16 strips, 1¾" × 42"; crosscut into:
    63 rectangles, 1¾" × 4½"
    8 strips, 1¾" × 41¼"
2 strips, 4" × 41¼"
3 strips, 4" × 42"

From the lime green solid, cut:
6 strips, 2½" × 42"

So Many Options!

You can make this quilt using Layer Cakes, 5" charm squares, or even small scraps. Simply cut individual 2½" squares and sew them together.

Assembling the Blocks

Press all seam allowances as shown by the arrows in the illustrations.

1. Sew two assorted 2½" × 10¼" strips together along the long edges to make a strip set. Press the seam allowances toward the darker fabric. Repeat for all 2½" × 10¼" strips to make 36 strip sets. Crosscut the strip sets into 144 segments, 2½" wide.

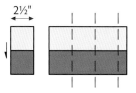

Make 36 strip sets. Cut 144 segments.

2 Sew two segments together as shown, placing them so that the seam allowances go in opposite directions. The completed Four Patch block should measure 4½" square, including seam allowances. Make 72 blocks.

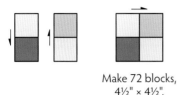

Make 72 blocks,
4½" × 4½".

Assembling the Quilt Top

1 Arrange eight blocks and seven cream print 1¾" × 4½" rectangles together into a row. Make nine rows, each beginning and ending with a Four Patch block.

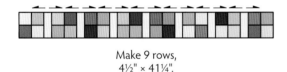

Make 9 rows,
4½" × 41¼".

2 Sew the rows together with a cream 1¾" × 41¼" sashing strip between each row.

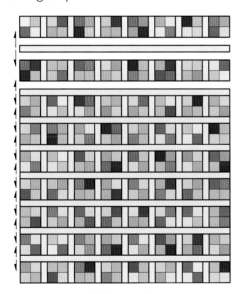

Quilt assembly

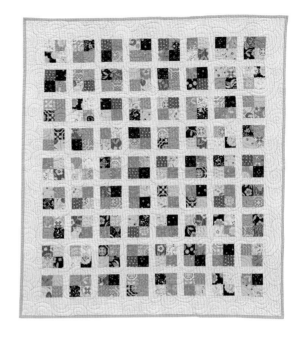

3 Sew the two cream 4" × 41¼" strips to the top and bottom of the quilt top. Press the seam allowances toward the center of the quilt.

4 Sew the three cream 4" × 42" strips together end to end with a diagonal seam. Press the seam allowances open. Measure the length of the quilt top through the center and cut two border strips to that measurement. Sew the strips to the sides of the quilt top. Press the seam allowances toward the center of the quilt. The finished quilt top should measure 48¼" × 53½".

Finishing the Quilt

For help with the following steps, go to ShopMartingale.com/HowtoQuilt for free, illustrated instructions.

1 Cut and piece the backing fabric so that it's 3" to 4" larger than the quilt top on all four sides.

2 Mark any quilting lines needed, and then layer the backing, batting, and quilt top. Baste the layers together and quilt. The quilt shown was quilted in an overall design of echoing spirals.

3 Trim the batting and backing even with the quilt top.

4 Use the lime green 2½"-wide strips to make and attach the binding.

Irish Heather

FINISHED QUILT: 60½" × 70½"
FINISHED BLOCK: 10" × 10"

This Irish Chain pattern is perfect for strips, whether you get them by raiding your stash or by purchasing an irresistible Jelly Roll. A scrappy Greek Cross comes together as a secondary design when the blocks are sewn together. Made with one simple block and no triangles, this is a great pattern for a novice quilter.

Materials

Yardage is based on 42"-wide fabric.

30 Jelly Roll strips, 2½" × 44", of assorted medium and dark prints for blocks*
1⅝ yards of cream print A for blocks
1⅝ yards of cream print B for blocks
⅝ yard of brown solid for binding
4¼ yards of fabric for backing
69" × 79" piece of batting

*After removing the selvage ends but before you start cutting pieces for blocks, measure your strips to make sure they are at least 42" long. If not, you may need to add strips.

Cutting

All measurements include ¼" seam allowances. Choose 14 strips for the Irish Chain and 16 strips for the corner units and cut as directed.

From *each of 14* medium or dark print strips for the Irish Chain, cut:
3 strips, 2½" × 10½" (42 total)
3 squares, 2½" × 2½" (42 total)

From *each of 16* medium or dark print strips for corner units, cut:
4 strips, 2½" × 10½" (64 total)

From cream print A, cut:
20 strips, 2½" × 42"; crosscut into:
    32 strips, 2½" × 10½"
    84 rectangles, 2½" × 4½"

From cream print B, cut:
20 strips, 2½" × 42"; crosscut into:
    32 strips, 2½" × 10½"
    84 rectangles, 2½" × 4½"

From the brown solid, cut:
7 strips, 2½" × 42"

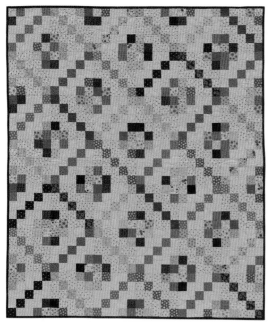

Designed by Sue Pfau, made by Heather Esmond

A Place for Everything

If you have any busy light-print strips or other strips that don't contrast strongly with the cream background prints, use them in step 1 to make the block corner units. If you position the light squares in the outer corners of the block, they'll be in the center of the Greek Cross that's created when the blocks are joined.

Assembling the Blocks

Press all seam allowances as shown by the arrows in the illustrations.

1 Sew two print 2½" × 10½" strips for the corner units together along the long edges to make a strip set. Press the seam allowances toward the darker strip. Make 21 strip sets. Crosscut each strip set into four segments, 2½" wide, for a total of 84.

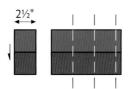

Make 21 strip sets.
Cut 4 segments from each.

2 Sew a print 2½" × 10½" strip for the corner unit and a cream 2½" × 10½" strip together along the long edges to make a strip set. Make 11 strip sets with cream A and 11 strip sets with cream B. Crosscut each strip set into four segments, 2½" wide, for a total of 88 (4 are extra).

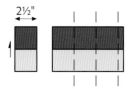

Make 11 strip sets with cream A
and 11 strip sets with cream B.
Cut 4 segments from each.

3 Sew a segment from step 1 and a segment from step 2 together to make a four-patch corner unit. Make 84 corner units that measure 4½" square, including seam allowances. Set these aside. You'll have 42 of each cream print.

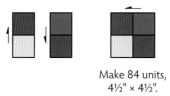

Make 84 units,
4½" × 4½".

4 Sew a print 2½" × 10½" strip for the Irish Chain and a cream strip together along the long edges to make a strip set. Crosscut the strip set into four segments, 2½" wide.

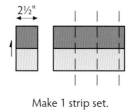

Make 1 strip set.
Cut 4 segments.

5 Sew the segments into a four-patch unit. Make two units that measure 4½" square, including seam allowances.

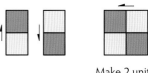

Make 2 units,
4½" × 4½".

6 Arrange four matching cream print 2½" × 4½" rectangles, the units from step 5, a print 2½" square that matches the units from step 5, and two corner units with cream print that matches the units from step 5 as shown. Sew the units together into rows, and then sew the rows together. The completed block should measure 10½" square, including seam allowances.

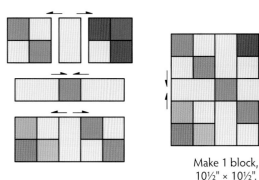

Make 1 block,
10½" × 10½".

7 Repeat steps 4–6 to make 21 blocks from each cream print, for a total of 42.

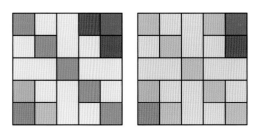

Make 21 of each.

Assembling the Quilt Top

Arrange the blocks in seven rows of six blocks each, alternating the cream blocks and rotating each block as indicated in the assembly diagram. Sew the blocks together into rows and then join the rows. The finished quilt top should measure 60½" × 70½".

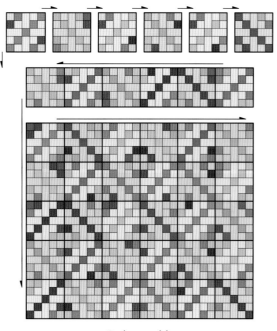

Quilt assembly

Finishing the Quilt

For help with the following steps, go to ShopMartingale.com/HowtoQuilt for free, illustrated instructions.

1 Cut and piece the backing fabric so that it's 4" larger than the quilt top on all four sides.

2 Mark any quilting lines needed, and then layer the backing, batting, and quilt top. Baste the layers together and quilt. The quilt shown was quilted with an overall design of feathers and swirls.

3 Trim the batting and backing even with the quilt top.

4 Use the brown 2½"-wide strips to make and attach the binding.

Scrappy Makes Me Happy

Jelly-Roll Friendly

FINISHED QUILT: 68½" × 68½"
FINISHED BLOCK: 8" × 8"

I love the latticework pattern formed throughout this quilt by the background fabric. The block is similar to a traditional Arkansas Crossroads design, but instead of only using the background fabric for the diagonal lattice, I also used it in the four-patch units and eliminated a few seams. This quilt is another great scrap buster. While it has a more complicated, on-point look, it's actually a simple horizontal layout. You really need medium and dark fabrics to show off the design, so pick your strips wisely!

Materials

Yardage is based on 42"-wide fabric.

32 Jelly Roll strips, 2½" × 42", of assorted medium and dark prints for blocks*
4 yards of low-volume cream print for blocks and border
⅔ yard of blue print for binding
4¾ yards of fabric for backing
77" × 77" piece of batting

*After removing selvage ends but before cutting pieces for blocks, measure your strips to make sure you have 41" of usable length. If not, you may need to add strips.

Cutting

All measurements include ¼" seam allowances.

From *each* of the 32 medium and dark print strips, cut:
2 strips, 2½" × 10¼" (64 total)
8 squares, 2½" × 2½" (256 total)

From the cream print, cut:
16 strips, 4½" × 42"; crosscut into 128 squares, 4½" × 4½"
23 strips, 2½" × 42"; crosscut 16 of the strips into 64 strips, 2½" × 10¼"

From the blue print, cut:
8 strips, 2½" × 42"

Mixing in Busy Lights

You want the Jelly Roll strips to contrast with the background fabric. If you need to include busy lights, as I did, cut them into four strips, 2½" × 10¼", for the four-patch units, and don't cut any squares. To compensate, cut a darker strip into 16 squares, making sure to end up with 64 strips and 256 squares.

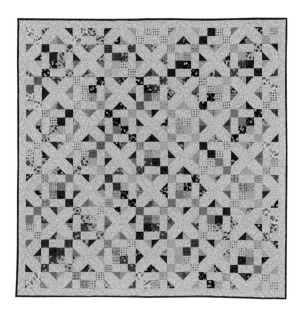

Assembling the Blocks

Press all seam allowances as shown by the arrows in the illustrations.

1 Sew together print and cream 2½" × 10¼" strips as shown to make 64 strip sets. Crosscut each strip set into four segments, 2½" wide, for a total of 256. Keep matching segments together.

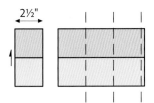

Make 64 strip sets.
Cut 4 segments from each.

2 Sew two matching segments into a four-patch unit. Make 128 units that measure 4½" square, including seam allowances.

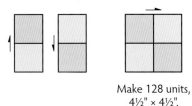

Make 128 units,
4½" × 4½".

3 Draw a diagonal line from corner to corner on the wrong side of the print 2½" squares. Place two marked print squares on opposite corners of a cream 4½" square. Sew on the drawn line. Trim the excess fabric in the corner, leaving a ¼" seam allowance. Press. Make 128 units that measure 4½" square, including seam allowances.

Make 128 units,
4½" × 4½".

4 Arrange two four-patch units from step 2 and two units from step 3 as shown. Sew the units together into rows, and then sew the rows together. The completed block should measure 8½" square, including seam allowances. Make 64 blocks.

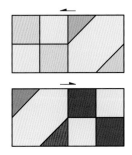 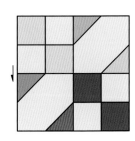

Make 64 blocks,
8½" × 8½".

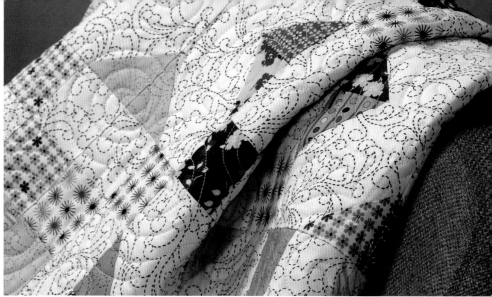

Assembling the Quilt Top

1 Arrange the blocks in eight rows of eight blocks each, rotating the blocks as shown in the assembly diagram to create the lattice design. Sew the blocks together into rows; join the rows.

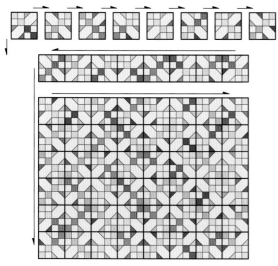

Quilt assembly

2 Join the remaining seven cream 2½" × 42" strips end to end with a diagonal seam. Press the seam allowances open. Measure the width of the quilt top through the center and cut two border strips to that measurement. Sew the strips to the top and bottom of the quilt top. Press the seam allowances toward the border.

3 Measure the length of the quilt top through the center and cut two border strips to that measurement. Sew the strips to the sides of the quilt top and press the seam allowances toward the border. The finished quilt top should measure 68½" square.

Finishing the Quilt

For help with the following steps, go to ShopMartingale.com/HowtoQuilt for free, illustrated instructions.

1 Cut and piece the backing fabric so that it's 4" larger than the quilt top on all four sides.

2 Mark any quilting lines needed, and then layer the backing, batting, and quilt top. Baste the layers together and quilt. The quilt shown was quilted in close swirls and flowers.

3 Trim the batting and backing even with the quilt top.

4 Use the blue 2½"-wide strips to make and attach the binding.

The Ties That Bind

FINISHED QUILT: 72½" × 72½"
FINISHED BLOCK: 12" × 12"

This quilt looks complex, but it's made with just one block. When multiplied across the quilt top, it creates amazing secondary designs. In fact, you can look at this quilt for hours and keep finding something new! Using a variety of low-volume background fabrics increases the appeal. Featuring just two main colors, the quilt's color scheme is easy to change to suit your taste. Red, white, and black is a popular combination, so I was able to buy a large Moda fat-quarter bundle plus just a few extra reds and creams to make it work.

Materials

Yardage is based on 42"-wide fabric.

5 fat quarters, 18" × 21", of assorted black prints for blocks

21 fat quarters of assorted cream and light gray prints for blocks*

9 fat quarters of assorted red prints for blocks

⅔ yard of charcoal print for binding

5 yards of fabric for backing

81" × 81" piece of batting

Many of the low-volume cream prints used in the quilt shown include red, gray, or black accents.

Cutting

All measurements include ¼" seam allowances.

From *each* of the 5 black fat quarters, cut:
6 strips, 2½" × 21" (30 total; 3 are extra)

From *each of 9* cream or gray fat quarters for chain units, cut:
2 strips, 4½" × 21" (18 total)
2 strips, 2½" × 21" (18 total)

From *each of 12* cream or gray fat quarters for bear-paw units, cut:
1 strip, 3" × 21"; crosscut into 6 squares, 3" × 3" (72 total)
4 strips, 2½" × 21"; crosscut into 30 squares, 2½" × 2½" (360 total)

From *each of the 9* red fat quarters, cut:
2 strips, 3" × 21"; crosscut into 8 squares, 3" × 3" (72 total)
4 strips, 2½" × 21"; crosscut into 16 rectangles, 2½" × 4½" (144 total)

From the charcoal print, cut:
8 strips, 2½" × 42"

Designed by Sue Pfau, made by Kristina Yelle

Assembling the Chain Units

Organize the black strips and the cream or gray strips into nine groups, each containing three matching black 2½" × 21" strips and a matching set of four cream or gray strips—two each of 4½" × 21" and 2½" × 21" strips. The cream or gray strips will be called simply "light" in the instructions.

Press all seam allowances as shown by the arrows in the illustrations.

1 Sew a light 4½" × 21" strip and a black 2½" × 21" strip together along the long edges to make a strip set. Make two matching strip sets and crosscut each into eight segments, 2½" wide, for a total of 16.

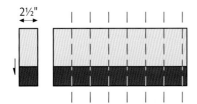

Make 2 strip sets. Cut 8 segments from each.

2 Sew a black 2½" × 21" strip between two matching light 2½" × 21" strips to make

a strip set. Crosscut the strip set into eight segments, 2½" wide.

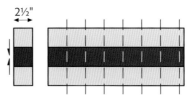

Make 1 strip set. Cut 8 segments.

3 Sew the segments together as shown. Make eight matching chain units and trim if necessary to measure 6½" square, including seam allowances. Keep the units together in matching pairs.

Make 8 units, 6½" × 6½".

4 Repeat steps 1–3 with the nine groups of black and light strips to make a total of 72 chain units.

Assembling Bear-Paw Units

For each pair of bear-paw units, you'll need:

- 2 red squares, 3" × 3", and 4 matching red rectangles, 2½" × 4½"

- 2 light squares, 3" × 3", and 10 matching light squares, 2½" × 2½"

Keep the units together in matching pairs.

1 Draw a diagonal line from corner to corner on the wrong side of the two light 3" squares. Pair a marked square with each red 3" square, right sides together. Sew a scant ¼" seam on each side of the diagonal line. Cut each square in half along the diagonal line and press to make four half-square-triangle units. Trim the units to measure 2½" square, including seam allowances.

Make 4 units.

2 Draw a diagonal line from corner to corner on the wrong side of four light 2½" squares. Place a marked square on one end of a red 2½" × 4½" rectangle, right sides together as shown. Sew on the line, trim the seam allowances to ¼", and press. Make two units with the diagonal going in one direction and two units with the diagonal going in the opposite direction.

Make 2 of each unit, 2½" × 4½".

3 Arrange two half-square-triangle units and two matching light 2½" squares as shown. Sew the units into rows. Sew the rows together. Make two units.

Make 2 units, 4½" × 4½".

4 Arrange two units from step 2, one unit from step 3, and a matching light 2½" square as shown. Sew the units into rows. Sew the rows together to make a bear-paw unit. Make two matching units.

Make 2 units, 6½" × 6½".

5 Repeat steps 1–4 with the 36 groups to make a total of 72 bear-paw units.

Assembling the Blocks

Arrange two matching chain units and two matching bear-paw units as shown. Sew the units in rows. Join the rows. The completed block should measure 12½" square, including seam allowances. Make 36 blocks.

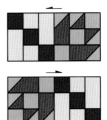 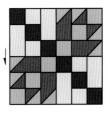

Make 36 blocks, 12½" × 12½".

Assembling the Quilt Top

Arrange the blocks in six rows of six blocks each as shown. Sew the blocks together into rows; then join the rows. The quilt top should measure 72½" square.

Quilt assembly

Finishing the Quilt

For help with the following steps, go to ShopMartingale.com/HowtoQuilt for free, illustrated instructions.

1 Cut and piece the backing fabric so that it's 4" larger than the quilt top on all four sides.

2 Mark any quilting lines needed. Layer and baste the backing, batting, and quilt top. Quilt. The quilt shown was quilted in an overall design of echoing spirals and flowers.

3 Trim the batting and backing even with the quilt top. Use the charcoal 2½"-wide strips to make and attach the binding.

Four Sisters

Fat-Quarter Friendly

FINISHED QUILT: 56¼" × 64¾"
FINISHED BLOCK: 8½" × 8½"

The Shuttle block always catches my eye. The four squares in the block center are a reminder of my Grandma Mary and her three sisters. They were very close-knit siblings who laughed constantly when they got together. I think you will find this quilt to be a nice size, and it goes together fast!

Materials

Yardage is based on 42"-wide fabric.

16 fat quarters, 18" × 21", of assorted prints for blocks and pieced outer border
1⅓ yards of cream print for blocks and inner border
⅝ yard of green print for binding
3¾ yards of fabric for backing
65" × 73" piece of batting

Cutting

All measurements include ¼" seam allowances. Divide the fat quarters into two groups: 8 for the "shuttles" and 8 for the squares and pieced border. If you have light print fat quarters, use them for the squares and pieced border. Cut the fat quarters and strips carefully to make sure you can cut all of the pieces. You will need a full 21" of usable fabric across the width.

From *each of 8* print fat quarters for shuttles, cut:
1 strip, 5¼" × 21"; crosscut into 4 squares, 5¼" × 5¼". Cut each square in half diagonally to make 8 triangles (64 total; 4 are extra).
3 strips, 2½" × 21"; crosscut into:
    4 strips, 2½" × 10½" (32 total; 2 are extra)
    2 strips, 2½" × 5¼" (16 total; 1 is extra)

From *each of 8* print fat quarters for squares, cut:
2 strips, 2½" × 21"; crosscut into:
    2 strips, 2½" × 10½" (16 total; 1 is extra)
    4 strips, 2½" × 5¼" (32 total; 2 are extra)

From the remainder of *1* print fat quarter, cut:
4 squares, 5" × 5"*

From the leftovers of the print fat quarters, cut a *total* of:
48 rectangles, 4¾" × 5"

From the cream print, cut:
6 strips, 2⅝" × 42"
5 strips, 5¼" × 42"; crosscut into 30 squares, 5¼" × 5¼". Cut each square in half diagonally to make 60 triangles.

From the green print, cut:
7 strips, 2½" × 42"

*These are for the border corner squares.

Assembling the Blocks

You will make two identical blocks at a time. For each pair of blocks, you'll need matching sets of:

- 2 strips, 2½" × 10½"; 1 strip 2½" × 5¼"; and 2 triangles for the shuttles

- 1 strip, 2½" × 10½", and 2 strips, 2½" × 5¼", for the squares

- 2 cream triangles

Press all seam allowances as shown by the arrows in the illustrations.

1 Sew the 2½" × 10½" strips together along the long edges as shown to make a strip set. Crosscut the strip set into four segments, 2½" wide.

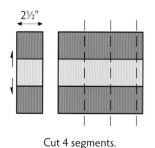

Cut 4 segments.

2 Sew the 2½" × 5¼" strips together along the long edges as shown to make a strip set. Crosscut the strip set into two segments, 2½" wide.

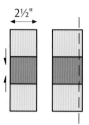

Cut 2 segments.

3 Sew the segments together to form two identical nine-patch units measuring 6½" square, including seam allowances.

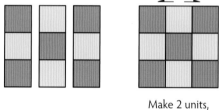

Make 2 units,
6½" × 6½".

4 Fold the nine-patch units and matching triangles in half and crease to mark the centers. Match the creased centers, right sides together, and sew the triangles to opposite sides of the nine-patch units. Trim the dog-ears from each unit. Make two.

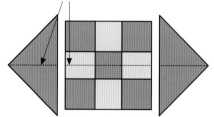

Match creased centers.

Make 2 units.

5 Repeat step 4 to sew cream triangles to the remaining sides of the nine-patch units. Trim the block if necessary to measure 9" square, including seam allowances, making sure to leave

a ¼" seam allowance beyond the points of the nine-patch units. Make 30 blocks.

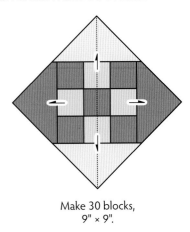

Make 30 blocks,
9" × 9".

Assembling the Quilt Top

1 Arrange the blocks in six rows of five blocks each. Sew the blocks together into rows, and then join the rows.

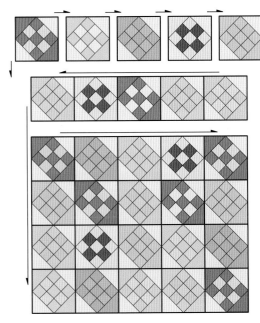

Quilt assembly

2 Sew the six cream 2⅝" × 42" strips together end to end with a diagonal seam. Measure the length of the quilt top through the center and cut two cream strips to that measurement. Sew the strips to the sides of the quilt top.

3 Measure the width of the quilt top through the center and cut two cream strips to that measurement. Sew the strips to the top and bottom

of the quilt top. The quilt top should measure 47¼" × 55¾", including seam allowances.

4 Sew together 13 of the 4¾" × 5" rectangles along the 5" sides. Make two strips that measure 5" × 55¾", including seam allowances, for the side borders. Sew together 11 of the rectangles and add a 5" square to each end of the strip. Make two strips that measure 5" × 56¼", including seam allowances, for the top and bottom borders. Press in one direction.

5 Sew the longer strips to the sides of the quilt top, and then sew the shorter strips to the top and bottom. The finished quilt top should measure 56¼" × 64¾".

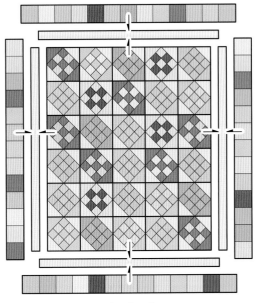

Adding borders

Finishing the Quilt

For help with the following steps, go to ShopMartingale.com/HowtoQuilt for free, illustrated instructions.

1 Cut and piece the backing fabric so that it's 4" larger than the quilt top on all four sides.

2 Mark any quilting lines needed, and then layer the backing, batting, and quilt top. Baste the layers together and quilt. The quilt shown was quilted in an overall design of echoing teardrops.

3 Trim the batting and backing even with the quilt top. Use the green 2½"-wide strips to make and attach the binding.

Churn Dash Echo

Fat-Quarter Friendly

FINISHED QUILT: 57½" × 57½"
FINISHED BLOCK: 14¼" × 14¼"

One of my favorite blocks is the Churn Dash. I also like the look of an "echoing" block, and this block design lends itself well to that idea. Picking out the colors for each block was so much fun! The fabrics give this quilt a happy, youthful look, but I think it would look striking in a variety of colors and fabrics. The block centers and backgrounds can show off your favorites.

Materials

Yardage is based on 42"-wide fabric.

24 fat quarters, 18" × 21", of assorted light, medium, and dark prints for blocks*
⅝ yard of navy print for binding
4 yards of fabric for backing
64" × 64" piece of batting

*Cut the fat quarters and strips carefully to make sure you can cut all of the pieces. You will need a full 21" of usable fabric across the width.

Cutting

All measurements include ¼" seam allowances.

From each of 16 print fat quarters (for the background and inner Churn Dash), cut:
1 strip, 1¾" × 21" (16 total)
1 strip, 2¾" × 21" (16 total)
2 squares, 5¾" × 5¾" (32 total)
1 square, 5¼" × 5¼" (16 total)
4 squares, 3" × 3" (64 total)

From each of 8 print fat quarters (for the outer Churn Dash), cut:
2 strips, 1¾" × 21" (16 total)

4 squares, 5¾" × 5¾" (32 total)

From the navy print, cut:
7 strips, 2½" × 42"

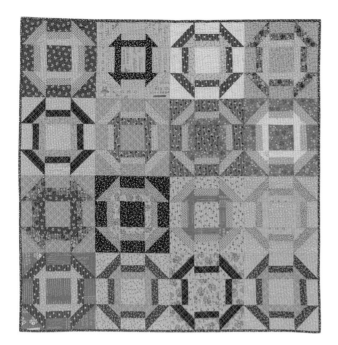

Press all seam allowances as shown by the arrows in the illustrations.

1 Draw a diagonal line from corner to corner on the wrong side of the two 5¾" squares of fabric A for the background. Pair each marked square with a 5¾" square of fabric B, right sides together. Sew a scant ¼" seam on each side of the diagonal line. Cut each square in half on the line and press. You'll have four identical half-square-triangle units. Trim each unit to measure 5¼" square, including seam allowances.

Make 4 units.

Assembling the Blocks

The instructions are written for making one block at a time. Each block is made up of three fabrics: fabric A for the block background, fabric B for the outer churn dash, and fabric C for the inner churn dash. For each block, you'll need:

Fabric A: A matching set of 1 strip, 2¾" × 21"; 2 squares, 5¾" × 5¾"; and 1 square, 5¼" × 5¼"
Fabric B: 1 strip, 1¾" × 21", and 2 matching squares, 5¾" × 5¾"
Fabric C: 1 strip, 1¾" × 21", and 4 matching squares, 3" × 3"

2 Draw a diagonal line from corner to corner on the wrong side of each 3" square of fabric C. Place a marked square on the fabric B corner of a half-square-triangle unit from step 1, right sides together. Sew on the diagonal line. Trim the excess fabric from the corner leaving a ¼" seam allowance. Press. Make four units.

Make 4 units.

3 Sew the B and C 1¾" × 21" strips together with the 2¾" × 21" strip of fabric A to make a strip set as shown. The fabric B strip should be in the middle. Crosscut the strip set into four segments, 5¼" wide.

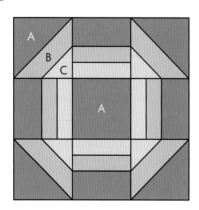

Fabric placement

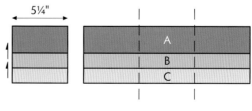

Cut 4 segments.

Assembling the Quilt Top

Arrange the blocks in four rows of four blocks each. Rotate each block so that the seam allowances in adjacent blocks are pressed in opposite directions. Sew the blocks together into rows, and then join the rows. The finished quilt top should measure 57½" square.

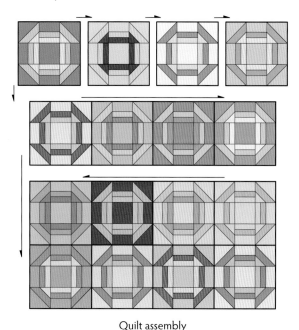

Quilt assembly

4 Arrange the four units from step 2, the segments from step 3, and the matching 5¼" square of fabric A as shown. Sew the units together into rows, and then sew the rows together. The completed block should measure 14¾" square, including seam allowances. Make 16 blocks.

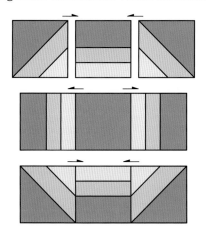

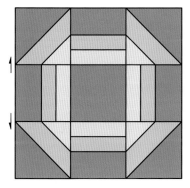

Make 16 blocks,
14¾" × 14¾".

Finishing the Quilt

For help with the following steps, go to ShopMartingale.com/HowtoQuilt for free, illustrated instructions.

1 Cut and piece the backing fabric so that it's 4" larger than the quilt top on all four sides.

2 Mark any quilting lines needed, and then layer the backing, batting, and quilt top. Baste the layers together and quilt. The quilt shown was quilted in an overall pattern of echoing spiral designs.

3 Trim the batting and backing even with the quilt top.

4 Use the navy 2½"-wide strips to make and attach the binding.

About the Author

Sue Pfau lives in the Adirondack Mountain region of upstate New York with her husband and two kids. When she's not busy sewing, she loves to spend time with her children and enjoys reading, gardening, and cooking. Sue learned to hand appliqué when she was a flight attendant looking for a satisfying hobby to fill her free time at work. After about five years she transitioned to machine piecing, and she hasn't looked back since! She left her airline job after she and her husband started a family, and as she cared for their daughter, Jane, she started looking for ways to keep busy at home and make a little extra money. That is how her business, Sweet Jane's, began.

In addition to writing two other books for Martingale, *Quilts from Sweet Jane* (2013) and *One Bundle of Fun* (2016), Sue has developed more than 90 patterns for quilts, bags, and small projects focusing on precut fabrics. She is also a regular contributor to *Quilting Quickly* magazine.

What's your creative passion?
Find it at ShopMartingale.com

books • eBooks • ePatterns • blog • free projects
videos • tutorials • inspiration • giveaways

Martingale®
Create with Confidence